Gymnastics Lessons Learned

Life Lessons through Gymnastics

Karen Goeller, CSCS

By Karen Goeller, CSCS

Gymnastics Lessons Learned

Life Lessons through Gymnastics

Karen Goeller, CSCS

ISBN-13: 978-1484013021
ISBN-10: 1484013026

This book is dedicated to all of the coaches who helped me through my earlier years and all of the gymnasts who have trained with me.

Over the past 30 years I have met so many amazing people in the sport of gymnastics and feel privelidged to have interracted with each of them.

And of course, my parents who have supported me throughout the years with my involvement in the sport and in life.

The names of the people in this book have been changed to protect their privacy.

Many of the illustrations are available on apparel and gifts at www.GymnasticsTees.com.

By Karen Goeller, CSCS

By Karen Goeller, CSCS   Copyright © Goeller

Reach for the Stars... With Your Toes!

One thing my Mom told me growing up was to never let anyone tell me that I can't do something. She also often said, "You can do anything you put your mind to." But Mom also knew that I struggled in school and worked very hard for my B average throughout grammar and high school. In college I had a variety of grades from A's to one F. Yup,

By Karen Goeller, CSCS

that one F hurt, big time. But it did not hold me back. Yes, Mom was right, never let anyone hold you back and you CAN do anything you set out to do.

Let me tell you the story of two gymnasts who had goals and so few adults took them seriously. Despite that, they both went far beyond their goals and most people's expectations.

A gymnast walked into my gymnastics facility and wanted to be on the team. She tried every other gymnastics facility in the area and no one took her seriously. She was already 14 years old and had a very serious goal, to compete in gymnastics. Sherry was overweight and weak. She could not do a push up or a handstand yet. Sherry and her Mom begged our coaches to take her seriously. I always remembered Mom's advice and felt I HAD to give Sherry a chance. We allowed her to train with the beginner group of girls in her age group to start. She excelled faster than any of them and slowly lost the excess weight. Within six weeks we invited Sherry to train with the next higher group. Sherry was the only one from that class invited to move up to the pre-team. Only six weeks and she has already begun to prove herself to the world. By that time, Sherry could not only perform a handstand, she could perform all of the skills required for level 5. Before we knew it, less than 6 months later Sherry competed level 5 and qualified to level 6. She was a happy and hard-working gymnast. She soon appeared strong, fit, and most importantly, happy! Sherry is one of many athletes who has proven adults wrong, reached her goals, and changed her life for the better. Not only was Sherry performing level 8 skills in less than one year of gymnastics, she learned that she can reach her goals and that no one could hold her back. The lessons Sherry, her teammates, and the entire staff of my gymnastics facility learned will be remembered forever.

Another gymnast, ten year old Carla, went to several gymnastics facilities within a 15 mile radius in and around NYC. She too wanted to compete in gymnastics and none of the other gymnastics coaches took her seriously. Some said she would never make it to the pre-team level. Well, we took her seriously and she ended up reaching level 10 and going on to compete in gymnastics for an Ivy League college. Carla came into the gym every day, listened to every word the coaches said, and made every skill, drill, and routine count. She gave her best effort every single day and every single moment during the workout. When I met Carla she could not do one pull-up on bars nor could she perform a pull-over. She could barely perform a handstand on floor. Within 5 years of training every day for 4 hours a day she reached level 10. Carla is a great example that you too should follow your dreams because they might really come true!

You too can reach for the stars... And no one can hold you back! Make small goals AND dream big because one day it will be your turn to succeed.

Your Success Depends on Your Effort...

Now keep in mind that there is only one person who can help you reach your goals, YOU!

After deciding what your goals are, you must figure out what is necessary to reach them. What will it take on a daily basis? The two gymnasts in the last chapter knew they had to find a coach to take them seriously. But they also knew they had to give their best effort, listen to every word

By Karen Goeller, CSCS

the coach said, and take care of their health at home in order to reach their goals.

You see, your parents, coaches, teachers, and the other adults in your life can only do so much. It is up to you to give your best effort with everything you try, whether it is a gymnastics routine, your homework, or anything else that is important in your life. Really dig deep and try your best with all of the necessary tasks required to reach your goals.

I'll tell you about another two gymnasts, one who did not make great efforts and the other who did. One gymnast who did not put in great efforts did not want to be in the gym. We'll call her Shelly. Shelly was there because her parents forced her to continue with the sport. At 13 years old and six years in the sport, she felt she had enough of the long hours and high demands of being a competitive gymnast. She intentionally did not try to perform at her best during skills, conditioning, or routines. Shelly chose to remain on the same level of competition so that she would not have to perform more difficult skills or a more intense workout. At this point Shelly wanted the easy way out. And by the end of the gymnastics season she paid for all of the time she wasted in the gym, the lack of effort, and the missed workouts. Shelly did not qualify to the state championships for the first time in four years. She was disappointed, complained, and she blamed everyone except for herself.

Her parents asked the coaches why their daughter performed so poorly at the last few meets. When I pulled out the notebook that documented the workouts and showed Shelly's parents how many skills and routines Shelly performed compared to the rest of the team girls, it all made sense. I told Shelly's parents that Shelly was informed many times that she might not reach her goals with her lack of effort and desire to train. Each time, Shelly shrugged her shoulders and walked away from me or the other coaches. She finished that season and ended up leaving the sport. Her parents finally realized that this was not the

sport for Shelly. A few months later, Shelly's parents contacted me. They told

me that she was happily training to compete in swimming and promised her

parents she would give it her best in her new sport.

Whether it is gymnastics, swimming, or some other sport it is up to you, to succeed.

On the other hand, there was nine year old Susy. She came in every day,

performed each conditioning exercise, skill, drill, and routine with great

efforts. She often asked what she did wrong so that she could improve her

performance. Susy listened to the coaches and tried very hard to make

corrections. And it was not always easy for her. Each day Susy wanted to be a

better gymnast than the previous day. At the end of the season, she not only

qualified to states, but she won uneven bars! Susy was the new state champion on uneven bars and had the best meet of her life. Susy was proof that your success depends on your effort, and not always your natural talent.

The coaches can only do so much. They are there to help, but if you do not try to do what they are saying, your progress might be slow.

Listen carefully to your coach's advice and give it your best because you too can succeed. And once you do, the feeling will be remembered forever.

Committed to Excellence...

And then there is excellence. Just trying to perform a skill is not always enough. And trying to make only one correction a day may not be enough. You must remember all of the recent corrections from your coach and try to keep the changes forever. You must try to perform each skill, drill, and routine as perfectly as you can. Always striving for perfection or excellence will give

By Karen Goeller, CSCS

you the best chance of progressing through the sport at a good rate, making future skills easier to learn. And you'll enjoy your high scores at meets if you do! Those high scores will make you feel the gratification for a long, long time.

Little Kay came into the gym as a level 4. She tried out for the team and I was quick with her evaluation. I asked her to perform a few skills and conditioning exercises on uneven bars then the real test began. I asked Kay to perform a plank. That is similar to a push-up position, but the forearm and hand are on the floor. I helped Kay get to the correct shape and then left her there. I was always within a few feet, but was not actively coaching her. Kay stayed in that shape for several minutes, until I told her to relax. That was the test. Kay was truly a one in one thousand type gymnast. I have only seen a few children with this amazing ability to listen and this much discipline over the past two decades. Kay has reached level 9 within a short time. And she is a high quality gymnast, scoring above 9.6 on all four events. Evidently, Kay is committed to excellence when she performs every skill, drill, and routine; that is why she receives near perfect scores at meets. Kay is very enthusiastic every day in the gym and she enjoys the challenges this sport offers.

You too can perform with excellence in the gym. When you are in the habit of striving for perfection, you will perform better, and enjoy the wonderful results.

By Karen Goeller, CSCS   Copyright © Goeller

Believe in Yourself...

You MUST believe you can reach your goals. How does that happen? Believing in yourself does not always come easy, but with the help of a good gymnastics coach, your supportive parents, and your strong desire to succeed confidence will become a habit. I have had many gymnasts that had difficulty with skills and lost their confidence. But when they conquered small

By Karen Goeller, CSCS   Copyright © Goeller

hurdles they began to change their mindset. Every day you should make small goals and celebrate when you achieve them. Maybe you can tell yourself that you will keep good form during your skills or stay on the beam during your routine. Whatever your daily or weekly goal is, remind yourself that you WILL reach it. Before you know it, you will be your own biggest fan. You will begin to believe in yourself once you see the smaller successes.

This next gymnast, Rina, had so much difficulty with vaulting that she wanted to quit gymnastics. She did some private training with me to help with vault. We figured out that it was her run and her lack of upper body flexibility. Once Rina's run became faster and her upper body was stretched correctly she noticed that her vault was getting easier. Vaulting seemed to become less stressful for her on a daily basis. Within only one month Rina went from being on the verge of quitting gymnastics to actually enjoying her new and improved vault. She performed her Yurechenko vault at the next meet and was thrilled with her score and overall experience. Rina started the gymnastics season with very little confidence, but was thrilled at her state meet. Her confidence improved and her love of the sport was renewed.

You too can reach your goals, believe in yourself, and renew your love of the sport.

I Can Do Anything...

You certainly can! And keep telling yourself that so that you will succeed in this sport and in anything else you try to accomplish in your life. Every gymnast struggles at one point or another so it is easy to forget that with hard work you will reach your goals. Your "struggle skill" might be a back walkover on beam, a giant on uneven bars, or maybe the full twisting Yurechenko. You must remember that if you struggle with the skill you must listen to your coaches and have faith that they

By Karen Goeller, CSCS

know when you are ready to perform it. Sometimes you must take the gulp and go for it. There may be a time when you get a weird gut feeling that things are not quite right and you must NOT go for the skill, but if is it just a slight discomfort and your coach is ready to spot you, it may be a good time to just do it.

Amanda struggled with her full twist on floor. Every time the coach asked her to perform the skill she would balk (not go). She kept telling herself she would get hurt. She really did not want to perform that skill (ever) or compete as a level 8.

In the beginning of the gymnastics season Amanda noticed that her teammate Katie also struggled with a skill on floor, her double back. But Katie was different than Amanda. Katie really, really wanted the skill and had big goals. She wanted a college scholarship one day. Katie told herself every day that she "could do anything." Katie continued to listen to her coaches, make the corrections they asked, and she performed the skill with the coach spotting her for two months. Katie knew she needed some more time to practice the double back with the coaches before she could easily perform it in a meet. After four months of saying aloud, "I can do anything!" Katie competed the double back in her floor routine. That was the happiest day she had in months. All of Katie's positive thinking and hard work paid off. This was a great lesson. As a result, Katie knows she will succeed at anything she tries in gymnastics and in life.

You too can reach your goals if you continue to believe in yourself, remind yourself that you CAN do anything, and really make great efforts towards reaching your goal. Focus on your smaller goals first and you will eventually meet that big goal. You CAN do anything, and you know it.

By Karen Goeller, CSCS

Dare to Dream...

Do you... Dare to dream? Do you hope that one day you will go to the Olympics or compete in college? Well then, you MUST keep your eye on your dream and keep working towards it every day. In 1976, when I was 10 years old, I had a dream. I was a gymnast in a YMCA with two really good coaches. That was the only place to do gymnastics in Brooklyn, NY. One day we were vaulting and my coach Willie told us to take a

By Karen Goeller, CSCS

short break. It was summer time and we were all dripping with sweat. He asked all of us this question, "If you had all the money in the world, what would you do with it?" I heard my teammates say they would buy a big house, an expensive car, and all sorts of luxury items.

Willie noticed that I was looking around the gym. He interrupted my great daydream! Willie asked me his question, "If you had all of the money in the world, what would you do with it?" I simply said, "I want my own gym." His response was, "Now that's a gymnast!" I really wanted the luxury of being able to swing on the bars and do back handsprings on the beam whenever I desired.

Throughout the years I told people that I was going to own a gymnastics club one day. No one believed me, but I knew it would happen. And at age 21, my childhood dream came true. I bought the gymnastics club that I worked in for several years. I cannot explain the amazing feeling it was to have a dream come true, but the feeling is like nothing else in the world. Years of wishing and working towards this dream finally paid off.

So, if you have a dream or a hefty goal, you must keep believing that it will happen. You must keep working towards that dream every day. And do not let anyone tell you that it is impossible or that it will not happen. I had many people along the way say it would never happen, but there were also those who believed in me. Those people are still in my life today.

You must follow your dreams because if you do not, you might really regret it later in life.

I had a second childhood dream, but that one did not come true. Something even BETTER happened. When I was a gymnast my Dad took me to watch the American Cup at Madison Square Garden in NYC. I watched the Olympic level gymnasts compete and wished I could be one of Bela Karolyi's gymnasts. I was

By Karen Goeller, CSCS   Copyright © Goeller

amazed with how easily they could perform so many difficult skills. I loved the sport and wanted to be an elite gymnast. That never happened due to chronic knee pain, tendonitis and Osgood.

In 1978, the doctor told me that there was nothing that could be done for my knee pain. My only option was to "quit gymnastics" to get rid of the pain. So, at 12 years old I stopped competing and started coaching. I went through the training program at the YMCA and completed it successfully. In 1978 I was given a few groups of young kids to coach. Within a short time I was coaching the pre-team, a group of 6-8 year old girls. Shortly after that, at age 12, I was hired by a private gymnastics club to coach a few classes. Yes, my coaching career has been LONG.

Getting back to my second dream, the one that did not EXACTLY happen... In 1989, I received a camp brochure and coaching contract in the mail from Bela

Karolyi. He was an Olympic coach. He was Nadia's and Mary Lou Retton's coach.

I was beyond thrilled to see this contract. I did not hesitate one moment. I signed the contract, bought my plane ticket, and counted down the days until I was on that plane to Texas.

This was even better than my childhood dream! I was able to work with with Bela Karolyi, learn from him, and use what I learned with my own gymnasts. I worked for Bela Karolyi for seven summers and was his first female camp director!

You see, dreams DO come true when you consistently work towards them and believe they will happen. Dream big… it just might happen!

By Karen Goeller, CSCS   Copyright © Goeller

Eat, Sleep, and Breathe Gymnastics

What does that mean? Do you love gymnastics so much that it is all you talk about? Is it the first thing you think of in the morning and the last thing you think about before you go to sleep? Do you dream about gymnastics when you sleep? Are you the first to arrive at the gym and the last to leave?

If so, you have found your passion in life. And maybe you should consider remaining in the sport as an adult.

By Karen Goeller, CSCS

It's very different for those who have a passion. The hard work is more tolerable and the workouts are more enjoyable. The challenges are fun and reaching your goals is exciting.

Not everyone on your team feels this way. Perhaps some of your teammates enjoy the sport, but they also enjoy other activities so they miss gym time. And others may complain about the challenges during the workout. Some of your teammates may be showing up at the gym simply because their parents want them to stay involved. They may not enjoy the sport and may not understand your passion.

Just remember, you must not let them bring your mood down or interrupt your great progress. Keep doing what you love. You'll be happy now and you'll be happy for many years to come. When you are an adult you will look back on your gymnastics years with good memories and thoughts. I can tell you that I certainly do!

I had one gymnast, Sue, who trained with me for 9 years. She absolutely loved the sport and had very big goals. Sue trained hard every day and did not get involved in the chalk bucket conversations. She was there to do gymnastics. Her fun was in getting a new skill or scoring high at a meet. She won bars, her favorite event, at many meets.

Sue loved being upside down as much as right side up! She never missed a practice and never wanted to leave the gym at night. Her Mom brought her dinner to the gym so that she could eat it before her long trip home because she knew that Sue would not leave if she was in the middle of a skill or routine. Gymnastics was Sue's life.

By Karen Goeller, CSCS   Copyright © Goeller

Sue is now a grown woman with a great career. I have kept in touch with her and her Mom for many years. One thing that made me feel great as a coach was when Sue said, "It was well worth it." She trained 24 hours a week with me and won Uneven Bars at age 16 at Level 10 Nationals many years ago.

If you truly love the sport, stay involved. You have found your passion so keep enjoying yourself. Life goes very fast. Throughout life, be sure to find time to do what you enjoy. You'll be a much happier person.

Accept the Challenge

Gymnastic is a difficult sport, but I know you're definitely up for the challenge.

Did you ever hear the old saying, "When the going gets tough, the tough get going?" Maybe you should keep that in mind when the workout gets really difficult. You must try even harder when it feels impossible. Dig deep, and give your best effort, especially when it gets tough. You'll like the results if you do!

By Karen Goeller, CSCS

I know a gymnast who worked harder and harder as I gave her more challenges. Maria came in as a very weak level 4 gymnast and left a level 10 state champion. She trained hard in the gym every day, and when I increased the difficulty, she rose to the occasion, every single time. Maria was the gymnast that every coach wanted to coach. She really tried to make corrections with skills and worked hard during conditioning.

Maria never missed a beat. She performed every skill, drill, and routine that I assigned with perfect form and as well as she could. Her hard work really paid off in the long run. She loved the sport and loved to compete. The challenges during training and the excitement at meets kept Maria on her toes. Not only did Maria win an event at level 10 states, she went on to compete for an Ivy League college. Her love of the sport and competing continued on throughout her college years.

Decide now. Accept the challenge and YOU will succeed. Look at a challenge as a goal that someone else sets for you. Try to look at challenges as fun puzzles or obstacles. With a positive outlook it will be easier to accept each challenge your coach offers and to succeed at the challenges.

Figure out how you can succeed, what you must do, listen to your coaches, come up with a plan, and work EVERY day to get through the challenge. Set goals, give it your best effort with everything you do, and you will be a success in gymnastics and life.

Hard Work Pays Off

Gymnastics Stuff TM

Hard work pays off...

We have all heard that saying, "Hard work pays off." Well, it really does... and I bet you know that already.

Whether you are trying to do well on an exam in school or get your personal best score at a meet, it will only happen if you put in the work. In school it is studying and in the gym it is repetitions. Not only should you be performing lots of numbers, but performing each skill, drill, and routine to the BEST of your ability.

So it's not only taking your turn on the equipment that counts, it's taking GOOD turns, really making every turn count.

By Karen Goeller, CSCS

And besides working hard, a gymnast must work smart. You must give great efforts, but also make sure you are using your time wisely. Perform every skill, drill, and routine that your coach asks and it will pay off in the long run. You'll feel good about the progress you make and you'll appreciate the moments when you finally reach your goal. Success is exciting!

I have seen countless gymnasts succeed, but the ones who impress me the most are those who deal with and recover from injuries like champions.

I had a parent contact me because her daughter, Carly, was a level 5 gymnast and broke her arm. It was a severe break, a compound fracture. Carly's Mom was very upset when she contacted me because she knew the road to recovery would be very long. It would be at least 12 weeks before Carly could be cleared for any weight bearing on that arm. The road back to doing gymnastics and competing was going to be a long, tough road. Carly's Mom knew she needed a gymnastics coach who was also very experienced with injuries.

I worked with Carly several times each week. I first met Carly a few days after the injury. The doctor said she would not be going to a physical therapist, but she could work with me through each step of healing process.

Carly had a cast that covered her entire arm, up to her shoulder. In the beginning she looked exhausted and weak. At first I just had Carly move her shoulder in a few different directions. She was able to shrug and perform small arm raises, lifting her arm (cast) forward and up. Carly soon progressed to holding a 1 pound weight in the other hand as she moved both shoulders and arms in several directions. The cast alone offered resistance so we wanted to make it even by using the light weight in the other hand.

We also did a great deal of work for Carly's legs and core. For several weeks we just trained at a comfortable level. Once the cast was removed and a shorter cast applied we started to train a little harder. Carly was in less pain and was much more comfortable with the idea of doing gymnastics conditioning.

By Karen Goeller, CSCS

Carly performed every exercise I asked and often performed more repetitions than I suggested. She focused on her form and the correct technique. At this point Carly was able to perform planks and other exercises from the prone position. Carly and her Mom were really thrilled that she could do so much with the short cast. Carly always rose to the challenge, even though she was uncomfortable with the cast on her arm.

When the cast was finally removed and a Velcro brace applied, we bumped up the intensity. By this point Carly was having fun with the conditioning and continually asked for a challenge.

Carly really loved the challenges and trained hard, often asking to perform more than the numbers I assigned. She was soon able to di weight bearing on her fist, keeping her wrist joint straight. At that point, Carly was holding a push up shape on her fists to develop strength and bone density.

Carly was on a mission and she knew she had to work hard to get her strength back and get back into competition shape. She followed my training system for regaining mobility and strength and continually surpassed each goal we set. It was exciting to see the progress and Carly celebrated each milestone with her Mom.

Carly's doctor was thrilled with her progress during each visit and Carly was ready for regular gymnastics training right on schedule. She reached her goals because she worked hard during our training sessions. She pushed herself through each repetition and accepted every challenge I offered. Her amazing progress would not have happened if Carly did not perform every repetition with her best effort and ask for more challenges each time.

You too can reach your goals if you work hard. But working hard is not all there is. Working smart is just as important. Try to work towards reaching your goals with your coach's guidelines in mind. It's true, hard work pays off. You'll see.

By Karen Goeller, CSCS

You Perform the Way You Practice

Did you know that? Your daily training is a good predictor of how well you will perform at a competition. How you practice on a daily basis will literally determine your success.

If you are in the gym every day giving great efforts, making corrections, and keeping good form you will likely be happy with your competition results.

By Karen Goeller, CSCS

But... if you are only giving half the effort you should, your competition scores will reflect that. And you will be unhappy with your scores and placement at the meet.

One gymnast, Marci, refused to listen to the coaches and never made any effort during practice. She performed her skills with poor form and carelessly threw her body around during skills. Marci just did not want to be in the gym. This poor work ethic and nonchalant practice went on for the entire summer and into competition season.

At the first meet Marci was blown away, not by her great scores, but by her LOW scores. Marci went home from the meet crying because she was shocked at the outcome, even though she was told every day that this could happen. The coaches encouraged Marci to work harder and train with the corrections in mind, but Marci just refused to listen and the results spoke for themselves.

It was a tough lesson learned for Marci and she returned to the gym the following week with a little more enthusiasm. She made more corrections during skills and tried to perform a little better. Her change in attitude helped and Marci performed better at her next meet.

So ask yourself whether you are training seriously or half-heartedly. If you are working with good form every day, you will have good form when you compete. But if you are practicing skills with bent knees or flexed feet your scores will reflect your bad form.

So remember, what you do during gym time greatly affects how well (or poorly) you will perform at competitions. The way you train will reveal your scores at meets. **Ask yourself how you are performing every day during training. And practice your routines in the gym as if you are competing every day. Try to remember that you will compete as well, or as poorly, as you practice. You**

By Karen Goeller, CSCS

will appreciate the result if you practice

as your coach asks you to practice.

Great Rewards Often Follow Great Efforts

Do you know that amazing feeling you get when you finally "get" a skill? Well, that high level of satisfaction and excitement are increased greatly when you continue on your path to reach your big goals.

It starts with small

By Karen Goeller, CSCS   Copyright © Goeller

goals and small rewards and then one day it may be your turn to be called champion.

Whether you reach the next level in gymnastics, qualify to States, win at National's, or make the Olympic team it all starts with great efforts in the gym every day and with every skill.

Dream big, but be sure to make short term goals along the way so that you can celebrate the special moments and smaller victories. Setting and reaching goals makes training so much more fun.

One of my gymnasts, Rebecca, made great efforts every day. Each day she came in with a goal, whether it was to improve a skill or stay on the beam, she had something in mind.

Most of the time she shared her goals with her teammates and coach. Other times she did not, but I often figured it out, especially when I saw her do her happy dance or a fist pump with a big smile. Rebecca enjoyed the whole process of learning skills and refining old skills every day. She loved gymnastics!

Her big meet was States. And guess what? She won two events, uneven bars and balance beam! You see, great efforts along with a good attitude every day will help you reach your goals. And you will be rewarded, whether it is by "getting" a skill or winning a big meet, there is always a reward of some sort.

Feeling the exhilaration of winning at a big meet or succeeding in some other way is a feeling that you will always remember. Give it your best, give great efforts every day in training and you will love the results.

By Karen Goeller, CSCS

Today's Training is Tomorrow's Performance

It's true, what you do today will effect your performance in the future. That is true for what is done when you first start gymnastics and what you do only a few weeks before your competition.

Your competition is a reflection of how well or how poorly you have trained over the course of time. Many young gymnasts do not fully understand this concept.

By Karen Goeller, CSCS   Copyright © Goeller

It is a difficult thing to understand because sometimes there is so much time before the next competition.

I had one gymnast, Ariana, who refused to make efforts as she performed specific drills for skills while waiting for her turn on the beam and on bars. She just did not believe that the drills would help her skills. Ariana was 11 years old and thought she knew more than the coaches. That was a big mistake.

Ariana was a level 8 gymnast who wanted to be a level 9, but did not want to train as seriosuly as her level 9 and 10 teammates. Ariana went to her first level 8 meet and was seriously defeated. She fell off the beam twice and she missed a giant on uneven bars. At that point in time, after coaching 25 years already, she was the first gymnast of mine to ever miss a giant on bars at a meet.

Arinan's parents were very disappointed, but not with the coaching because they were kept up to date on our daily workouts. There were several times I called Araina's parents during workout so they could speak with her and remind her that she must listen to the coaches. That went on for much of the summer and into the competition season. The phone call helped a little. At the very least, her parents knew what was happening in the gym.

One day, something clicked and Araina started to train a little more seriously. I think she had a concersation with a relative who positively influenced her attitude. That change was just in time, six weeks before level 8 states.

Ariana did well at states, her all around score went up by 2 whole points and it was her best meet ever! She not only had the best meet of her life, Ariana qualified to Regionals! The efforts she made trying to correct skills in her routines really paid off. The next season Aiana competed level 9 and eventually got onto a college team.

By Karen Goeller, CSCS   Copyright © Goeller

It is never too late to train more seriously to improve your performance.

You'll be happy with your performance later if you prepare now and train

with diligence.

Believe and Achieve...

Do you believe you can reach YOUR gymnastics and life goals? If not, you MUST change that.

You must picture yourself every day as the gymnast you want to be. Whether you want to be a level 6 gymnast, a TOPS gymnast, or a college level gymnast you MUST believe that it can happen.

Or if you want to perform a certain gymnastics skill such as a

By Karen Goeller, CSCS

double full on floor or a layout on beam, you MUST picture yourself performing the skill you want to perform.

Little Jena wanted to be on the TOPS team more than anything. She knew what she had to do. She listened to the coaches instructions every day, and did everything she needed outside the gym in order to succeed. Even though Jena was only 8 years old, she asked her parents and coaches about healthy foods, she drank plenty of fluids, and she even went to bed as soon as her parents asked her so that she would wake up fresh and ready for her day.

Jena wanted to make every day a good day so that she could reach her goals. When she was in the gym she pretended she was at the TOPS tryouts and when she was home she was resting as her coaches instructed her to do. Jena played piano often when she was at home. That was great because she was resting her body, but exercising her mind.

In the gym, as Jena performed her cast handstands she asked her teammates and coaches to count. When she did her sprints she asked her coaches to use the stopwatch. Every day Jena believed she would make that team and every day she trained as if she was ALREADY a TOPS gymnast.

Three months later, Jena was on her way to the testing. In the car on the way to the TOPS testing, Jena told her parents that she was ready and would make the team. Jena's parents loved her confidence and encouraged her to do her best and have fun every day.

Once at the TOPS testing Jena was all smiles and ready to focus. She encouraged her teammates and continued stay positive throughout the event. Before Jena performed each exercise, her coach said, "Do it the same way you have been doing it in the gym. Stay focused, keep it going."

By Karen Goeller, CSCS

Before each turn Jena was saying, "believe, believe, believe." She said it three times each time she was about to be tested. The coaches who tested the gymnasts thought Jena's positive outlook was wonderful.

Jena knew this day was what she has been working towards. After each test she asked her coach how she did. Jena's belief in herself over the past three months, her hard work, and her love of the sport are the reasons Jena performed well at the testing.

Jena qualified to the TOPS Team and was more than thrilled. When her coach told her and her teammates that all three of them "made it to the TOPS team." They all jumped up and down and hugged each other in excitement. Jena blurted out, see, we believed we could do it!

You can reach your goals with a positive attitude, a belief that you can accomplish anything, and lots of hard work. When you believe in yourself it

makes a big difference in your training and your results. Picture yourself as the gymnast you want to be. You must imagine yourself reaching the goal you have in mind and you will do it too!

To Be a Champion... Train Like a Champion

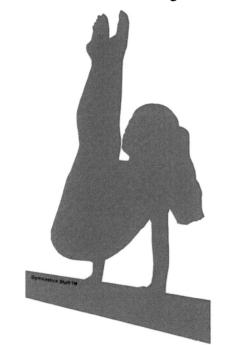

To be a champion...

You must train like a champion.

When you go into the gym to practice do you feel like a champion? Do you feel that you can reach your goals, come in 1st place, or make it to the elite level? And do you train as if you are already a champion every day?

When I had my gymnastics club we had an amazing choreographer and coach that worked with the team, Renville. Every time he trained them he said, "Look like a champion, act like

By Karen Goeller, CSCS

a champion, and train like a champion. Then you will BE a champion." Our gymnasts had very serious goals and they listened to his advice carefully.

One gymnast, Ella, was new to the team. She came in from another gymnastics club. Ella's previous coaches said that her skills were sloppy, she fooled around too much, and she only wanted to get to level 8. She was a very different gymnast than the girls on our team so I was not sure if she would survive the one week trial I offered her.

On Ella's first day she had the opportunity to train with Renville. He brought out the best in her right away. Ella was nothing like what her previous coaches said she was like. She spent the week training seriously and making great corrections. At the end of her one week trial week I asked Ella how she liked our gym and what her goals were.

Ella said she loved our workouts and never knew she had to pretend to be a champion already. Ella stayed with us and continued to train as if she was already the state champion on every event. A few months after Ella joined us she pictured herself as the level 10 National Champion often and even told her teammates they could all be champions. What a difference in her attitude and thinking. She just needed the right atmosphere and coaching.

Ella really bought into Renville's training philosophy and it helped her big time! Four years after Ella joined our team she competed at level 10 states and won floor! She won at countless meets along the way, but the level 10 state meet was her long term goal. Ella competed in Regionals and Nationals as well.

Within two years, Ella went on to compete for an Ivy League college. She believed she was a champion and trained as if she was a level 10 gymnast every

By Karen Goeller, CSCS   Copyright © Goeller day, long before she actually reached that level. That type of mental training paid off for Ella because she performed well when it counted the most.

Go into the gym every day ready for a good workout... your hair tied up tight, your leotard clean, your snack and drink in your bag, and your good attitude. Be ready to train as if you are already the champion, whether it is level 5 or elite. **Take every skill, drill, and routine seriously. You will make great progress and compete well if you act, look, and train like a champion.**

It's Not Just a Sport. It's My Life...

That was me growing up... I wanted to be in the gym ALL the time, I wanted to practice gymnastics at home so much that I bought my own gymnastic mat and I wanted my own gymnastics club ever since I was 10 years old.

By Karen Goeller, CSCS

It really has been my LIFE since the 1970's. I have coached many gymnasts who have reminded me of myself growing up. They too wanted to be in the gym all the time and really LIVED the sport.

Two of my gymnasts come to mind when I think of this quote. One was the gymnast in this illustration and the other is still in touch with me. They were BOTH level 10 National Champions, one on beam and one on bars. They had nothing in common other than the fact that they both came into the gym every day and trained seriously. They were both the first to arrive, the last to leave, and they took the most turns on the equipment.

One was a bars hog and one was a beam hog. It's no coincidence that those were the events they won at many meets from level 6-10. They both trained 24 hours each week and made tremendous progress each year. You see, that is what it takes not only reach high levels in gymnastics, but to be successful in life.

You MUST love the sport if you want to survive and thrive on the higher levels. You must make it your LIFE if you want to compete well on the higher levels.

Ask yourself how you feel about this sport and choose your goals based on your feelings. Be realistic, but dream big if this really is your LIFE. Be sure to share your goals with your coaches and parents so they can help you along the way.

It's
Not
Just
a
Sport.

It's
My
Life.

GymnasticsStuff.com

By Karen Goeller, CSCS   Copyright © Goeller

Visualize then Realize...

Did you know that mental training is just as important as physical training? Visualization takes time to learn and practice long before it is mastered.

Lisa was a level 9 gymnast and was quickly becoming a master at visualization. She came to me from another gym where they did not discuss focus or visualization. In order to get to level 9, Lisa had a good idea on how to focus, but she never took it as

By Karen Goeller, CSCS   Copyright © Goeller

far as picturing herself performing skills before taking her turn on the equipment.

Once she went through the process of learning visualization she was able to acquire skills more easily and performed them with more confidence. Visualization really worked well for Lisa when she was learning blinds and front giants on uneven bars. We went through the whole process of watching videos of elite gymnasts executing the skills to her visualizing herself performing the skill, long before Lisa actually did the skill on her own.

For several weeks I only had Lisa perform drills with her visualization practice. Only six weeks later Lisa added both skills into her uneven bars routine along with a forward flipping dismount. Her uneven bars score skyrocketed! She performed well at states, regionals, and the Eastern national meets!

Visualization often works really well when you are trying to learn a new skill. You must be able to visualize yourself performing the new skill over and over again.

One great way to learn to use visualization is to watch a short video clip of the skill and then close your eyes and replay the video in your mind. (Make sure the video you are watching is being performed by a gymnast with excellent technique.) Do that several times, run the video and picture the video. Once you can clearly see the picture in your mind of the video you just watched, picture yourself performing a skill that you have been performing for many years, such as a cartwheel. Once you can do that really well visualize yourself performing more difficult skills. Go through that process of watching a video clip and visualizing many times until you have mastered visualization. It may take several weeks to months for some gymnasts to master visualization.

You'll see, once you master visualization you will get skills much more quickly. You will also feel more confident performing the new skills.

Gymnastics… It's What I Do…

Is gymnastics just something you do or is it really WHO you are?

Let's define gymnastics or the qualities of a "gymnast"

Perseverance, determination, integrity, hard-working, persistent, driven, positive attitude, highly motivated, goal-oriented, and successful to name a few.

By Karen Goeller, CSCS

I would guess that if you have read this book you are a GYMNAST by all accounts! Keep up the hard work, keep setting goals, and keep going after what YOU want. Set short term and long term goals. Set small goals and big goals. And do not be afraid to DREAM BIG…

I sincerely hope you reach all of your gymnastics and life goals. Let me know how I can help you… www.KarenGoeller.com

Books by Karen Goeller

- Lymphedema: Sentenced to Life in Bed, but I Escaped
- Fitness on a Swing Set
- Fitness on a Swing Set with Training Programs
- Swing Set Workouts
- Gymnastics Drills and Conditioning Exercises
- Handstand Drills and Conditioning Exercises
- Gymnastics Drills: Walkover, Limber, Back Handspring
- Gymnastics Conditioning for the Legs and Ankles
- Gymnastics Journal: My Scores, My Goals, My Dreams
- Most Frequently Asked Questions about Gymnastics
- Fitness Journal: My Goals, Training, and Success
- Strength Training Journal
- Gymnastics Conditioning: Five Conditioning Workouts
- Gymnastics Conditioning: Tumbling Conditioning

Karen has also written countless articles and training programs.

www.GymnasticsBooks.com
www.KarenGoeller.com

By Karen Goeller, CSCS

About Karen Goeller

Karen Goeller, CSCS, has educated thousands in the fitness and gymnastics industries with her books, articles, and in person. She has been training athletes since 1978 and adults since 1985.

Karen Goeller enjoys helping athletes prepare for competition with specific conditioning and return to competition shape after an injury. She has helped athletes return to competitive shape after knee surgery, elbow surgery, fractures, rotator cuff and labrum tears, and tendonitis among other injuries. She regularly includes injury prevention exercises in her conditioning programs because she believes it is better to prevent injury than to rehab from one.

Karen Goeller is the author of more gymnastics books than anyone in the USA. Since the beginning Karen Goeller's books have been used as references by fitness experts and coaches to create countless training programs. Her books have been called the "most useful on the market."

When she was involved in an accident in 2000 and suffered permanent spinal damage she stopped working. To remain involved in gymnastics and fitness, Karen turned to writing. "I felt like I had a ton of information in my head that was not being used. I knew it was the perfect time to pass on this knowledge and writing books was the perfect avenue."

By Karen Goeller, CSCS   Copyright © Goeller

It wasn't until the Swing Set Fitness books that Karen started to make great progress with her physical rehabilitation. Karen shared, "I finally felt like myself again. I knew I was getting stronger, mentally and physically." When asked if she is completely healed from the accident, Karen replied, "I am still injured, but that no longer defines me."

Karen has produced State Champions, National TOPS Team Athletes, and Empire State Games Athletes. Three National Champions were from Karen's gymnastics club.

Most of her success was after her 1991 cancer surgery. Before her surgery, Karen was told that she would be bed-ridden for the rest of her life by many doctors. The cancer surgery was a success, but Karen was left with lymphedema in her leg. Her leg was as wide as her waist immediately after the surgery. Karen has written a book on her life since the surgery, "Lymphedema: Sentenced to Life in Bed, but I Escaped."

Karen Goeller and her athletes have been featured on TV, radio, and in the newspapers since the 1990's. She has appeared on Good Morning America, GoodDay NY, Eyewitness News, and NY Views (old show) among others. They have also been featured in The NY Times, NY Newsday, Brooklyn Bridge Magazine, and Interview Magazine, and most of the Brooklyn, NY newspapers.

More recently Karen has been featured on Cosmic Broadcasting, Erin Ley Radio, Your Story Matters Radio, Lymphedema Mavens Radio, Lynn Johnson Radio, I Run MY Body Radio, Late Night with Johnny Potenza TV, Talkin' Health with Joe Kasper Radio, the Coast Star, Asbury Park Press, Observer/Reporter, Staten Island Advance, and Inside Gymnastics Magazine among others.

Karen has worked for world famous Olympic coach, Bela Karolyi and was the first female camp director.

Before earning her BA Degree, Karen's education included training as an EMT, Physical Therapist, and Nutritionist. She has had certifications such as EMT-D, Nutritional Analysis, Fitness Trainer, many USAG certifications, and the NSCA-CSCS certification.

Karen is available for sports conditioning clinics, interviews, book signings, and consulting work. Her contact information is on her website.

www.KarenGoeller.com

61829452R00049

Made in the USA
San Bernardino, CA
15 December 2017